Lent: [illegible] towards the Resurrection

Pope Benedict XVI

All booklets are published thanks to the generous support of the members of the Catholic Truth Society

CATHOLIC TRUTH SOCIETY
PUBLISHERS TO THE HOLY SEE

Contents

Meeting the Justice of God in Jesus Christ 3

The Birth of a New Nature in us 9

A Universal Desire for Life 14

Spiritual Renewal in Lent 19

The Way of Repentance 24

Our Relationship with God 28

The Rules of Love 33

Living the days of the Easter Triduum 42

The Oil of Gladness 46

The Words of Jesus at the Last Supper 54

Resurrection Transforms the Cross 62

The Medicine of Immortality .65

The First Gift of the Holy Spirit 72

Meeting the Justice of God in Jesus Christ

Each year, on the occasion of Lent, the Church invites us to a sincere review of our life in light of the teachings of the Gospel. This year, I would like to offer you some reflections on the great theme of justice, beginning from the Pauline affirmation: "*The justice of God has been manifested through faith in Jesus Christ*" (cf. *Rm* 3, 21-22).

Justice: "dare cuique suum"

First of all, I want to consider the meaning of the term "justice," which in common usage implies "to render to every man his due," according to the famous expression of Ulpian, a Roman jurist of the third century. In reality, however, this classical definition does not specify what "*due*" is to be rendered to each person. What man needs most cannot be guaranteed to him by law. In order to live life to the full, something more intimate is necessary that can be granted only as a gift: we could say that man lives by that love which only God can communicate since He created the human person in His image and likeness. Material goods are certainly useful and required – indeed Jesus Himself was concerned to heal the sick, feed the crowds that followed Him and surely condemns the indifference that even today forces hundreds of millions into death through lack of food, water and medicine – yet -

distributive" justice does not render to the human being the totality of his "*due*." Just as man needs bread, so does man have even more need of God. Saint Augustine notes: if "justice is that virtue which gives every one his due ... where, then, is the justice of man, when he deserts the true God?" (*De civitate Dei*, XIX, 21).

What is the cause of Injustice?

The Evangelist Mark reports the following words of Jesus, which are inserted within the debate at that time regarding what is pure and impure: "There is nothing outside a man which by going into him can defile him; but the things which come out of a man are what defile him … What comes out of a man is what defiles a man. For from within, out of the heart of man, come evil thoughts" (*Mk* 7, 14-15, 20-21). Beyond the immediate question concerning food, we can detect in the reaction of the Pharisees a permanent temptation within man: to situate the origin of evil in an exterior cause. Many modern ideologies deep down have this presupposition: since injustice comes "from outside," in order for justice to reign, it is sufficient to remove the exterior causes that prevent it being achieved. This way of thinking – Jesus warns – is ingenuous and shortsighted. Injustice, the fruit of evil, does not have exclusively external roots; its origin lies in the human heart, where the seeds are found of a mysterious cooperation with evil. With bitterness the Psalmist recognises this: "Behold, I was brought forth in iniquity, and in sin did my mother conceive me" (*Ps* 51,7). Indeed, man is weakened by an intense influence, which wounds his capacity to enter into communion with the other. By nature, he is open to sharing freely, but he finds in his being a strange force of gravity that makes him turn in and affirm himself above and against others: this is egoism, the result of original sin. Adam and Eve, seduced by Satan's lie, snatching the mysterious fruit against the divine command, replaced the logic of trusting in Love with that of suspicion and competition; the logic of receiving and trustfully expecting from the Other with anxiously seizing and doing on one's own (cf. *Gn* 3, 1-6), experiencing, as a consequence, a sense of disquiet and uncertainty. How can man free himself from this selfish influence and open himself to love?

Justice and Sedaqah

At the heart of the wisdom of Israel, we find a profound link between faith in God who "lifts the needy from the ash heap" (*Ps* 113,7) and justice towards one's neighbour. The Hebrew word itself that indicates the virtue of justice, *sedaqah*, expresses this well. *Sedaqah*, in fact, signifies on the one hand full acceptance of the will of the God of Israel; on the other hand, equity in relation to one's neighbour (cf. *Ex* 20, 12-17), especially the poor, the stranger, the orphan and the widow (cf. *Dt* 10, 18-19). But the two meanings are linked because giving to the poor for the Israelite is none other than restoring what is owed to

God, who had pity on the misery of His people. It was not by chance that the gift to Moses of the tablets of the Law on Mount Sinai took place after the crossing of the Red Sea. Listening to the Law presupposes faith in God who first "heard the cry" of His people and "came down to deliver them out of hand of the Egyptians" (cf. *Ex* 3,8). God is attentive to the cry of the poor and in return asks to be listened to: He asks for justice towards the poor (cf. *Sir* 4,4-5, 8-9), the stranger (cf. *Ex* 22,20), the slave (cf. *Dt* 15, 12-18). In order to enter into justice, it is thus necessary to leave that illusion of self-sufficiency, the profound state of closure, which is the very origin of injustice. In other words, what is needed is an even deeper "exodus" than that accomplished by God with Moses, a liberation of the heart, which the Law on its own is powerless to realize. Does man have any hope of justice then?

Christ, the justice of God

The Christian Good News responds positively to man's thirst for justice, as Saint Paul affirms in the Letter to the Romans: "But now the justice of God has been manifested apart from law … the justice of God through faith in Jesus Christ for all who believe. For there is no distinction; since all have sinned and fall short of the glory of God, they are justified by His grace as a gift, through the redemption which is in Christ Jesus, whom God put forward as an expiation by his blood, to be received by faith" (3, 21-25). What then is the justice of Christ? Above all, it is the justice that comes from grace, where it is not man who makes amends, heals himself and others. The fact that "expiation" flows from the "blood" of Christ signifies that it is not man's sacrifices that free him from the weight of his faults, but the loving act of God who opens Himself in the extreme, even to the point of bearing in Himself the "curse" due to man so as to give in return the "blessing" due to God (cf. *Gal* 3, 13-14). But this raises an immediate objection: what kind of justice is this where the just man dies for the guilty and the guilty receives in return the blessing due to the just one? Would this not mean that each one receives the contrary of his "due"? In reality, here we discover divine justice, which is so profoundly different from its human counterpart. God has paid for us the price of the exchange in His Son, a price that is truly exorbitant. Before the justice of the Cross, man may rebel for this reveals how man is not a self-sufficient being, but in need of Another in order to realize himself fully. Conversion to Christ, believing in the Gospel, ultimately means this: to exit the illusion of self-sufficiency in order to discover and accept one's own need – the need of others and God, the need of His forgiveness and His friendship. So we understand how faith is altogether different from a natural, good-feeling, obvious fact: humility is required to accept that I need Another to free me from "what is mine," to give me gratuitously "what is His." This happens especially in the sacraments of Reconciliation and the Eucharist. Thanks to Christ's action, we may enter into the "greatest" justice, which is that of love (cf. *Rm* 13, 8-10), the justice that recognises itself in every case more a debtor than a creditor, because it has received more than could ever have been expected. Strengthened by this very experience, the Christian is moved to contribute to creating just societies, where all receive what is necessary to live according to the dignity proper to the human person and where justice is enlivened by love.

Dear brothers and sisters, Lent culminates in the Paschal Triduum, in which this year, too, we shall celebrate divine justice – the fullness of charity, gift, salvation. May this penitential season be for every Christian a time of authentic conversion and intense knowledge of the mystery of Christ, who came to fulfill every justice. With these sentiments, I cordially impart to all of you my Apostolic Blessing.

The Birth of a New Nature in us

Today, Ash Wednesday, we are beginning the Lenten Journey, a journey that takes 40 days and brings us to the joy of the Lord's Pasch. On this spiritual journey we are not alone because the Church accompanies and supports us from the outset with the word of God, which contains a programme of spiritual life and penitential commitment, and with the grace of the sacraments.

The Apostle Paul's words give us a precise order "We entreat you not to accept the grace of God in vain... Behold, now is the acceptable time; behold, now is the day of salvation" (2 *Cor* 6: 1-2).

Indeed in the Christian vision of life every moment must be favourable and every day must be a day of salvation but the Church's Liturgy speaks of this in a very special way in the Season of Lent. And we can understand that the 40 days in preparation for Easter are a favourable time and a time of grace precisely from the appeal that the austere rite of the imposition of ashes addresses to us and which is expressed in the Liturgy in two formulas: "Turn away from sin and be faithful to the Gospel"; "Remember, man, you are dust and to dust you will return".

The appeal for conversion

The first appeal is for conversion, a word to be understood with its extraordinary gravity, grasping the surprising newness it releases. The appeal to conversion, in fact, lays bare and denounces the facile superficiality that all too often marks our lives. To repent [or convert] is to change direction in the journey of life: not, however, by means of a small adjustment, but with a true and proper about turn. Conversion means swimming against the tide, where the "tide" is the superficial lifestyle, inconsistent and deceptive, that often sweeps us long, overwhelms us and makes us slaves to evil or at any rate prisoners of moral mediocrity. With conversion, on the other hand, we are aiming for the high standard of Christian living, we entrust ourselves to the living and personal Gospel which is Jesus Christ. He is our final goal and the profound meaning of conversion, he is the path on which all are called to walk through life, letting themselves be illumined by his light and sustained by his power which moves our steps. In this way conversion expresses his most splendid and fascinating Face: it is not a mere moral decision that rectifies our conduct in life, but rather a choice of faith that wholly involves us in close communion with Jesus as a real and living Person. To repent and believe in the Gospel are not two different things or in some way only juxtaposed, but express the same reality. Repentance is the total "yes" of those who consign their whole life to the Gospel responding freely to Christ who first offers himself to humankind as the Way, the Truth and the

Life, as the only One who sets us free and saves us. This is the precise meaning of the first words with which, according to the Evangelist Mark, Jesus begins preaching the "Gospel of God": "The time is fulfilled, and the Kingdom of God is at hand; repent, and believe in the Gospel" (*Mk* 1: 15).

Every day is a moment of grace

The "Repent, and believe in the Gospel" is not only at the beginning of Christian life but accompanies it throughout, endures, is renewed and spreads, branching out into all its expressions. Every day is a favourable moment of grace because every day presses us to give ourselves to Jesus, to trust in him, to abide in him, to share his lifestyle, to learn true love from him, to follow him in the daily fulfilment of the Father's will, the one great law of life. Every day, even when it is fraught with difficulties and toil, weariness and setbacks, even when we are tempted to leave the path of the following of Christ and withdraw into ourselves, into our selfishness, without realizing our need to open ourselves to the love of God in Christ, to live the same logic of justice and love. In my recent Message for Lent I wanted to recall that "humility is required to accept that I need Another to free me from "what is mine', to give me gratuitously "what is His'. This happens especially in the sacraments of Reconciliation and the Eucharist. Thanks to Christ's action, we may enter into the "greatest' justice, which is that of love (cf. *Rom* 13: 8-10), the justice that recognizes itself in every case more a debtor than a creditor, because it has received more than could ever have been expected" (*Message*, 30 October 2009).

Realism and wisdom in the face of death

The favourable moment of grace in Lent also reveals its spiritual significance to us in the ancient formula: "Remember, man, you are dust and to dust you will return" which the priest says as he places a little ash on our foreheads. Thus we are referred back to the dawn of human history when the Lord told Adam, after the original sin: "In the sweat of your face you shall eat bread till you return to the ground, for out of it you were taken; you are dust, and to dust you shall return" (*Gen* 3: 19). Here, the word of God reminds us of our frailty, indeed of our death, which is the extreme form. Before the innate fear of the end and even sooner in the context of a culture which in so many ways tends to censure the reality and the human experience of death, the Lenten Liturgy, on the one hand, reminds us of death, inviting us to realism and wisdom; but, on the other, it impels us above all to understand and live the unexpected newness that the Christian faith releases from the reality of death itself.

Man is dust and to dust he shall return, but dust is precious in God's eyes because God created man, destining him to immortality. Hence the Liturgical formula, "Remember, man, you are dust and to dust you will return", finds the fullness of its meaning in reference to the new Adam, Christ. The Lord Jesus also chose freely to share with every human being the destiny of weakness, in particular through his death on the Cross; but this very death, the culmination of his love for the Father and for humanity, was the way to the glorious Resurrection, through which Christ became a source of grace, given to all who believe in him, who are made to share in divine life itself. This life that will have no end has already begun in the earthly phase of our existence but it will be brought to completion after "the resurrection of the flesh". The little action of the imposition of ashes reveals to us the unique riches of its meaning. It is an invitation to spend the Lenten Season as a more conscious and intense immersion in Christ's Paschal Mystery in his death and Resurrection, through participation in the Eucharist and in the life of charity, which is born from the Eucharist in which it also finds its fulfilment. With the imposition of ashes we renew our commitment to following Jesus, to letting ourselves be transformed by his Paschal Mystery, to overcoming evil and to doing good, in order to make our former self, linked to sin die and to give birth to our "new nature", transformed by God's grace.

Dear friends, while we prepare to set out on the austere Lenten journey, let us invoke with special trust the protection and help of the Virgin Mary. May it be her, the first believer in Christ, to accompany us in these 40 days of intense prayer and sincere penitence so that we may arrive purified and completely renewed in mind and in spirit at the great Mystery of the Pasch of his Son. I wish you all a good Lent!

A Universal Desire for Life

"Lord, you are merciful to all, and hate nothing you have created. You overlook the sins of men to bring them to repentance. You are the Lord our God" (*Entrance Antiphon*). With this moving invocation from the Book of Wisdom (cf. 11: 23-26), the Liturgy opens the Eucharistic Celebration of Ash Wednesday. In a certain way, these words introduce the entire Lenten journey; they establish the omnipotence of God's love as the basis, his absolute dominion over every creature which is expressed in infinite forgiveness and animated by the constant, universal desire for life. Indeed, forgiving someone is equivalent to telling him or her: I do not want you to die, but to live; I always and only want the best for you.

Obedience to merciful love

This absolute certainty sustained Jesus during the 40 days he spent in the Judean desert, after he had received Baptism from John in the Jordan. For him that long period of silence and fasting was a complete abandonment of himself to the Father and to his plan of love. The time was a "baptism" in itself, that is, an "immersion" in God's will and in this sense a foretaste of the Passion and of the Cross. Going out into the desert alone to remain there at length meant exposing himself willingly to the assaults of the enemy, the tempter who brought about Adam's fall and whose envy caused death to enter the world (cf. *Wis* 2: 24). It meant engaging in battle with him, with nothing but the weapon of boundless faith to challenge him, in the omnipotent love of the Father. Your love is enough for me, my food is to do your will (cf. *Jn* 4: 34): this conviction pervaded Jesus' mind and heart during his time of "Lent". It was neither an act of pride nor a titanic undertaking but rather a humble choice, consistent with the Incarnation and the Baptism in the Jordan, in the same vein of obedience to the merciful love of the Father, who "so loved the world that he gave his only Son" (*Jn* 3: 16).

Assent to salvation

Our Lord Jesus did all this for us. He did it to save us, and at the same time to show us the path on which to follow him. Salvation is in fact a gift; it is the grace of God, but in order for it to make an impact on my life it requires my assent, an acceptance that is demonstrated in my actions in other words, the will to live like Jesus, to follow him. Following Jesus into the Lenten desert is therefore a prerequisite for participating in his Pasch, in his "exodus". Adam was banished from the earthly Paradise, a symbol of communion with God. Now, in order to return to this communion and thus to true life, to eternal life, it is necessary to cross the desert, the trial of faith not alone, but with Jesus! He has preceded us, as always, and has already won the battle against the spirit of evil. This is the meaning of Lent, the liturgical Season that every year invites us to renew our decision to follow Christ on the path of humility, in order to take part in his victory over sin and death.

Humility

In this perspective one can also understand the penitential symbol of the ashes, which are placed upon the heads of all those who begin the Lenten journey with good will. It is essentially an act of humility that means: I recognize myself for what I am, a frail creature, made from earth and destined to return to earth, yet also made in the image of God and destined for him. I am dust, yes, but also beloved, shaped by his love, animated by his vital breath, able to recognize his voice and respond to him. I am free and therefore capable of disobeying him, of giving in to the temptation of pride and self-sufficiency. This is sin, the deadly illness that came so soon to pollute the blessed earth that is the human being. Created in the image of the Holy and the Just, man lost his own innocence. Now he can only return to being just by the grace of God's justice, the justice of love that, as St Paul writes, "has been manifested... through faith in Jesus Christ" (cf. *Rom* 3: 21-22). These words of the Apostle provided an inspiration for the Message I addressed to all the faithful for this Lent, which is a reflection on the theme of justice in the light of the Sacred Scriptures and their fulfilment in Christ.

Sincerely repentant hearts

The theme of justice is also very present in Ash Wednesday's biblical readings. First, the passage from the prophet Joel and the Responsorial Psalm the Miserere form a penitential diptych. This highlights what the Bible calls "iniquity" that is, sin, which fundamentally consists in disobeying God, which means a lack of love as the origin of every material and social injustice. "For I know my transgressions", the Psalmist confesses, "and my sin is ever before me. Against you, you only, have I sinned, and done that which is evil in your sight" (*Ps* 51[50]: 3-4). The first act of justice is therefore recognizing one's own iniquity and realizing that it is rooted in the "heart", at the very core of the human person. The "fasting", "weeping" and "mourning" (cf. *Jl* 2: 12), and any other expression of penitence only have value in God's eyes if they are signs of sincerely repentant hearts.

The Gospel, too, taken from the "Sermon on the Mount", insists on the need to practice one's own "justice" almsgiving, prayer, fasting so that it may not be seen by men but only by the eyes of God, who "sees in secret" (cf. *Mt* 6: 1-6, 16-18). The true "reward" is not the admiration of others but rather friendship with God and the grace that derives from it, a grace that gives peace and strength to do good, to love even those who are not worthy, to forgive those who have offended us.

Love

The Second Reading, Paul's appeal to be reconciled to God (cf. 2 *Cor* 5: 20), contains one of the celebrated Pauline paradoxes, which leads to the whole reflection on justice in the mystery of Christ. St Paul writes, "For our sake he made him to be sin who knew no sin" that is, his Son made Man "so that in him we might become the righteousness of God" (2 *Cor* 5: 21). In Christ's heart, in other words at the core of his divine and human Person, the entire drama of freedom was played out in decisive and definitive terms. God took his own plan of salvation to extreme consequences, remaining faithful in his love even at the price of sending his only Son to death, to death on the Cross. As I wrote in my Lenten Message, "Here we discover divine justice, which is so profoundly different from its human counterpart.... Thanks to Christ's action, we may enter into the "greatest' justice, which is that of love (cf. *Rom* 13: 8-10)".

Spiritual Renewal in Lent

Temptations

Last Wednesday, with the penitential Rite of Ashes we began Lent, a Season of spiritual renewal in preparation for the annual celebration of Easter. But what does it mean to begin the Lenten journey? The Gospel for this First Sunday of Lent illustrates it for us with the account of the temptations of Jesus in the desert. The Evangelist St Luke recounts that after receiving Baptism from John, "Jesus, full of the Holy Spirit, returned from the Jordan, and was led by the Spirit for forty days in the wilderness, tempted by the devil" (*Lk* 4: 1). There is a clear insistence on the fact that the temptations were not just an incident on the way but rather the consequence of Jesus' decision to carry out the mission entrusted to him by the Father to live to the very end his reality as the beloved Son who trusts totally in him. Christ came into the world to set us free from sin and from the ambiguous fascination of planning our life leaving God out. He did not do so with loud proclamations but rather by fighting the Tempter himself, until the Cross. This example applies to everyone: the world is improved by starting with oneself, changing, with God's grace, everything in one's life that is not going well.

Material need

The first of the three temptations to which Satan subjects Jesus originates in hunger, that is, in material need: “If you are the Son of God command this stone to become bread". But Jesus responds with Sacred Scripture: “Man shall not live by bread alone” (*Lk* 4: 3-4; cf. Dt 8: 3). Then the Devil shows Jesus all the kingdoms of the earth and says: all this will be yours if, prostrating yourself, you worship me. This is the deception of power, and an attempt which Jesus was to unmask and reject: “You shall worship the Lord your God, and him only shall you serve” (cf. *Lk* 4: 5-8; Dt 6: 13). Not adoration of power, but only of God, of truth and love. Lastly, the Tempter suggests to Jesus that he work a spectacular miracle: that he throw himself down from the pinnacle of the Temple and let the angels save him so that everyone might believe in him. However, Jesus answers that God must never be put to the test (cf. *Dt* 6: 16). We cannot “do an experiment” in which God has to respond and show that he is God: we must believe in him! We should not make God “the substance” of “our experiment". Still referring to Sacred Scripture, Jesus puts the only authentic criterion obedience, conformity to God's will, which is the foundation of our existence before human criteria. This is also a fundamental teaching for us: if we carry God's word in our minds and hearts, if it enters our lives, if we trust in God, we can reject every kind of deception by the Tempter. Furthermore, Christ's image as the new Adam emerges clearly from this account. He is the Son of God, humble and obedient to the Father, unlike Adam and Eve who in the Garden of Eden succumbed to the seduction of the evil spirit, of being immortal without God.

Weapons of faith

Lent is like a long "retreat" in which to re-enter oneself and listen to God's voice in order to overcome the temptations of the Evil One and to find the truth of our existence. It is a time, we may say, of spiritual "training" in order to live alongside Jesus not with pride and presumption but rather by using the weapons of faith: namely prayer, listening to the Word of God and penance. In this way we shall succeed in celebrating Easter in truth, ready to renew our baptismal promises. May the Virgin Mary help us so that, guided by the Holy Spirit, we may live joyfully and fruitfully this Season of grace.

TRANSFIGURATION

On this Second Sunday of Lent the Liturgy is dominated by the episode of the Transfiguration which in Luke's Gospel immediately follows the Teacher's invitation: "If any man would come after me, let him deny himself and take up his cross daily and follow me" (*Lk* 9: 23). This extraordinary event is an encouragement in the following of Christ.

Luke does not speak of the Transfiguration but describes what happens through two elements: the Face of Jesus which changes and his clothes that become a dazzling white in the presence of Moses and Elijah, a symbol of the Law and of the Prophets. The three disciples who witness the scene are heavy with sleep: this is the attitude of those who, although they have seen divine miracles, fail to understand. It is only the struggle against drowsiness that enables Peter, James and John to "see" Jesus in his glory. Then the rhythm quickens: while Moses and Elijah take their leave of the Master, Peter speaks and as he speaks a cloud envelops him and the other disciples in its shadow. This cloud, while it covers them, reveals the glory of God, just as happened for the pilgrim people in the desert. Their eyes can no longer see but their ears can hear the voice that comes out of the cloud: "This is my Son, my Chosen; listen to him!" (v. 35).

The disciples no longer have before them a transfigured face or dazzling garments or a cloud that reveals the divine presence. They have before them "Jesus... alone" (v. 36). Jesus is alone with his Father while he prays but at the same time, "Jesus... alone" is all that the disciples and the Church of every epoch have been granted; and this must suffice on the journey. The only voice to listen to, the only voice to follow is his, the voice of the One going up to Jerusalem who was one day to give his life to "change our lowly body to be like his glorious body" (*Phil* 3: 21).

"Master, it is well that we are here" (*Lk* 9: 33) are Peter's ecstatic words, that often resemble our own desire before the Lord's consolations. However the Transfiguration reminds us that the joys sown by God in life are not finishing lines; rather they are lights he gives us during our earthly pilgrimage in order that "Jesus alone" may be our Law and his word the criterion that directs our existence.

In this Lenten period I invite everyone to meditate assiduously on the Gospel. I also hope that in this Year for Priests Pastors may be "truly pervaded by the word of God... really know that word... to the point that it really leaves a mark on [their] lives and shapes [their] thinking" (cf. *Homily, Chrism Mass*, 9 April 2009). May the Virgin Mary help us to live intensely our moments of encounter with the Lord so that we may follow him joyfully every day. Let us turn our gaze to her, invoking her with the prayer of the *Angelus*. I wish you all a good Sunday!

The Way of Repentance

"'Repent', says the Lord, "for the Kingdom of Heaven is at hand'", we proclaimed before the Gospel of this Third Sunday of Lent that presents us with the fundamental theme of this "strong season" of the liturgical year: the invitation to change our lives and to do works worthy of penance.

Jesus, as we heard, recalls two items of news: a brutal repression in the Temple by the Roman police (cf. *Lk* 13: 1) and the tragic death of 18 people, killed when the tower in Siloam collapsed (v. 4). People interpret these events as divine punishment for those victims' sins, and thinking they are upright, believe they are safe from such accidents and that they have nothing in their own lives that they should change. Jesus, however, denounces this attitude as an illusion: "Do you think that these Galileans were worse sinners than all the other Galileans, because they suffered thus? I tell you, no; but unless you repent you will all likewise perish" (vv. 2-3). And he invites us to reflect on these events for a greater commitment on the journey of conversion, for it is precisely the closure of ourselves to the Lord and the failure to take the path of our own conversion that lead to death, to the death of the soul. In Lent, each one of us is asked by God to mark a turning point in our life, thinking and living in accordance with the Gospel, correcting some aspect of our way of praying, acting or working and of our relations with others. Jesus makes this appeal to us, not with a severity that is an end in itself but precisely because he is concerned for our good, our happiness and our salvation. On our part, we must respond to him with a sincere inner effort, asking him to make us understand which particular ways we should change.

The prospect of mercy

The conclusion of the Gospel passage reverts to the prospect of mercy, showing the urgent need to return to God, to renew life in accordance with God. Referring to a custom of the time, Jesus presents the parable of a fig tree planted in the vineyard. However, this fig tree was barren, it produced no fruit (cf. *Lk* 13: 6-9). The dialogue that develops between the master and the vinedresser shows on the one hand the mercy of God who is patient and allows human beings, all of us, time in which to convert; and on the other, the need to start to change both our interior and exterior way of life straight away in order not to miss the opportunities that God's mercy affords us to overcome our spiritual laziness and respond to God's love with our own filial love.

Moreover, in the passage we have heard, St Paul urges us not to deceive ourselves: it is not enough to have been baptized and nourished at the Eucharistic table if we do not live as Christians and are not attentive to the Lord's signs (cf. 1 *Cor* 10: 1-4) ...

The burning bush of the cross

Dear brothers and sisters, the strong season of Lent invites each one of us to recognize the mystery of God that becomes present in our life, just as we heard in the First Reading. Moses sees a bush in the wilderness that is burning but without being consumed. First of all impelled by curiosity, he approaches it to see the mysterious event when suddenly a voice comes from the bush that says: "I am the God of your father, the God of Abraham, the God of Isaac, and the God of Jacob" (*Ex* 3: 6). And it is precisely this God who sent him to Egypt, charging him to lead the People of Israel to the Promised Land and to ask the Pharaoh, on his behalf, to set Israel free. At this point Moses asks God what his Name is, the Name with which God manifests his special authority, in order to present God to the people and then to the Pharaoh. God's answer may seem strange; it seems both an answer and not an answer. He says of himself simply: "I am who I am". "He is", and this must suffice. God, therefore, does not reject Moses' request. He pronounces his Name, thus creating the possibility of invoking him, of calling on him, of a relationship with him. By revealing his Name, God establishes a relationship between himself and us. He enables us to invoke him, he enters into relations with us and gives us the possibility of being in a relationship with him. This means that he gives himself, in a certain way, to our human world, becoming accessible, as if he were one of us. He faces the risk of the relationship, of being with us. What began in the burning bush in the desert is accomplished in the burning bush of the Cross where God, having become accessible in his Son made man, really became one of us, is put into our hands and, in this way, realizes the liberation of humanity. On Golgotha God, who during the night of the flight from Egypt revealed himself as the One who frees us from slavery, revealed himself as the One who embraces every human being with the saving power of the Cross and the Resurrection and liberates him from sin and death, accepts him in the embrace of his love.

Let us remain in contemplation of this mystery of God's Name, the better to understand the mystery of Lent and to live as individuals and as communities in permanent conversion, so as to be a constant epiphany in the world, a witness of the living God who sets us free us and saves us out of love. Amen.

Our Relationship with God

God the Father of mercy

On this Fourth Sunday of Lent, the Gospel of the father and the two sons better known as the Parable of the "Prodigal Son" (*Lk* 15:11-32) is proclaimed. This passage of St Luke constitutes one of the peaks of spirituality and literature of all time. Indeed, what would our culture, art and more generally our civilization be without this revelation of a God the Father so full of mercy? It never fails to move us and every time we hear or read it, it can suggest to us ever new meanings. Above all, this Gospel text has the power of speaking to us of God, of enabling us to know his Face and, better still, his Heart. After Jesus has told us of the merciful Father, things are no longer as they were before. We now know God; he is our Father who out of love created us to be free and endowed us with a conscience, who suffers when we get lost and rejoices when we return. For this reason, our relationship with him is built up through events, just as it happens for every child with his parents: at first he depends on them, then he asserts his autonomy; and, in the end if he develops well he reaches a mature relationship based on gratitude and authentic love.

Two immature ways of relating to God

In these stages we can also identify moments along man's journey in his relationship with God. There can be a phase that resembles childhood: religion prompted by need, by dependence. As man grows up and becomes emancipated, he wants to liberate himself from this submission and become free and adult, able to organize himself and make his own decisions, even thinking he can do without God. Precisely this stage is delicate and can lead to atheism, yet even this frequently conceals the need to discover God's true Face. Fortunately for us, God never fails in his faithfulness and even if we distance ourselves and get lost he continues to follow us with his love, forgiving our errors and speaking to our conscience from within in order to call us back to him. In this parable the sons behave in opposite ways: the younger son leaves home and sinks ever lower whereas the elder son stays at home, but he too has an immature relationship with the Father. In fact, when his brother comes back, the elder brother does not rejoice like the Father; on the contrary he becomes angry and refuses to enter the house. The two sons represent two immature ways of relating to God: rebellion and childish obedience. Both these forms are surmounted through the experience of mercy. Only by experiencing forgiveness, by recognizing one is loved with a freely given love a love greater than our wretchedness but also than our own merit do we at last enter into a truly filial and free relationship with God.

Dear friends, let us meditate on this parable. Let us compare ourselves to the two sons and, especially, contemplate the Heart of thc Father. Let us throw ourselves into his arms and be regenerated by his merciful love. May the Virgin Mary, *Mater Misericordiae*, help us to do this.

The Divine legislator

We have reached the Fifth Sunday of Lent in which the Liturgy this year presents to us the Gospel episode of Jesus who saves an adulterous woman condemned to death (*Jn* 8: 1-11). While he is teaching at the Temple the Scribes and Pharisees bring Jesus a woman caught in the act of adultery for which Mosaic law prescribed stoning. Those men ask Jesus to judge the sinful woman in order "to test him" and impel him to take a false step. The scene is full with drama: the life of that person and also his own life depend on Jesus. Indeed, the hypocritical accusers pretend to entrust the judgement to him whereas it is actually he himself whom they wish to accuse and judge. Jesus, on the other hand, is "full of grace and truth" (*Jn* 1: 14): he can read every human heart, he wants to condemn the sin but save the sinner, and unmask hypocrisy. St John the Evangelist highlights one detail: while his accusers are insistently interrogating him, Jesus bends down and starts writing with his finger on the ground. St Augustine notes that this gesture portrays Christ as the divine legislator: in fact, God wrote the law with his finger on tablets of stone (cf.

Commentary on John's Gospel, 33,5). Thus Jesus is the Legislator, he is Justice in person. And what is his sentence? "Let him who is without sin among you be the first to throw a stone at her". These words are full of the disarming power of truth that pulls down the wall of hypocrisy and opens consciences to a greater justice, that of love, in which consists the fulfilment of every precept (cf. *Rom* 13: 8-10). This is the justice that also saved Saul of Tarsus, transforming him into St Paul (cf. *Phil* 3: 8-14).

Sacramental pardon

When his accusers "went away, one by one, beginning with the eldest", Jesus, absolving the woman of her sin, ushers her into a new life oriented to good. "Neither do I condemn you; go, and do not sin again". It is the same grace that was to make the Apostle say: "One thing I do, forgetting what lies behind and straining forward to what lies ahead. I press on toward the goal for the prize of the upward call of God in Christ Jesus" (*Phil* 3: 13-14). God wants only goodness and life for us; he provides for the health of our soul through his ministers, delivering us from evil with the Sacrament of Reconciliation, so that no one may be lost but all may have the opportunity to convert. In this Year for Priests I would like to urge Pastors to imitate the holy Curé d'Ars in the ministry of sacramental pardon so that the faithful may discover its meaning and beauty and be healed by the merciful love of God, who "even forces himself to forget the future so that he can grant us his forgiveness!"

(*Letter to Priests for the Inauguration of the Year for Priests*, 16 June 2009).

Dear friends, let us learn from the Lord Jesus not to judge and not to condemn our neighbour. Let us learn to be intransigent with sin starting with our own! and indulgent with people. May the holy Mother of God, free from all sin, who is the mediatrix of grace for every repentant sinner, help us in this.

The Rules of Love

The Gospel of the blessing of the palms that we have heard gathered here in St Peter's Square, begins with the sentence: "[Jesus] went on ahead, going up to Jerusalem" (*Lk* 19: 28). At the very beginning of today's Liturgy, the Church anticipates her response to the Gospel saying: "Let us follow the Lord". This clearly expresses the theme of Palm Sunday. It is the *sequela*. Being Christian means considering the way of Jesus Christ as the right way for being human as that way which leads to our destination, to a completely fulfilled and authentic humanity. In a special way I would like to repeat to all young people on this 25th World Youth Day that being Christian is a path or, better, a pilgrimage; it is to travel with Jesus Christ, to journey in the direction he has pointed out and is pointing out to us.

The true heights of being human

But what direction is this? How do we find it? Our Gospel passage offers two clues in this regard. In the first place it says that it is an ascent. This has first of all a very concrete meaning. Jericho, where the last part of Jesus' pilgrimage began, is 250 metres below sea-level, whereas Jerusalem the destination is located at 740 to 780 metres above sea level: a climb of almost 1,000 metres. But this external route is above all an image of the internal movement of existence that occurs in the following of Christ: it is an ascent to the true heights of being human. Man can choose an easy path and avoid every effort. He can also sink to the low and the vulgar. He can flounder in the swamps of falsehood and dishonesty. Jesus walks before us and towards the heights. He leads us to what is great, pure. He leads us to that healthy air of the heights: to life in accordance with the truth; to courage that does not let itself be intimidated by the gossip of prevalent opinions; to patience that bears with and sustains the other. He guides people to be open towards the suffering, to those who are neglected. He leads us to stand loyally by the other, even when the situation becomes difficult. He leads us to the readiness to give help; to the goodness that does not let itself be disarmed, even by ingratitude. He leads us to love he leads us to God.

Jesus "went on ahead, going up to Jerusalem". If we interpret these words of the Gospel in the context of the way Jesus took in all its aspects a journey which, precisely, continues to the end of time in the destination, "Jerusalem", we can discover various levels indicated. Of course, first of all, it must be understood that this simply means the place, "Jerusalem": it is the city in which God's Temple stood, whose uniqueness must allude to the oneness of God himself. This place, therefore, proclaims two things: on the one hand it says that there is only one God in all the world, who exceeds by far all our places and times; he is that God to which the entire creation belongs. He is the God whom all men and women seek in their own depths, and of whom, in a certain way, they all have some knowledge. But this God gave himself a Name. He made himself known to us, he initiated a history with human beings; he chose a man Abraham as the starting point of this history. The infinite God is at the same time the close God. He, who cannot be confined to any building, nevertheless wants to dwell among us, to be totally with us.

Definite freedom

If Jesus, with the pilgrim Israel, goes up to Jerusalem, he goes there to celebrate with Israel the Passover: the memorial of Israel's liberation a memorial which, at the same time, is always a hope of definitive freedom, which God will give. And Jesus approaches this feast in the awareness that he himself is the Lamb in which will be accomplished what the Book of Exodus says in this regard: a lamb without blemish, a male, who at sunset, before the eyes of the children of Israel, is sacrificed "as an ordinance for ever" (cf. *Ex* 12: 5-6, 14). And lastly, Jesus knows that his way goes further: the Cross will not be his end. He knows that his journey will rend the veil between this world and God's world; that he will ascend to the throne of God and reconcile God and man in his Body He knows that his Risen Body will be the new sacrifice and the new Temple; that around him, from the hosts of Angels and Saints the new Jerusalem will be formed, that is in Heaven and yet also on the earth, because by his Passion he was to open the frontier between Heaven and earth. His way leads beyond the summit of the Mountain of the Temple to the heights of God himself: this is the great ascent to which he calls us all. He always remains with us on earth and he has always already arrived with God. He guides us on earth and beyond the earth.

The humility of being roped together

Thus, the dimensions of our *sequela* become visible in the ascent of Jesus the goal to which he wants to lead us: to the heights of God, to communion with God, to being-with-God. This is the true destination and communion with him is the way to it. Communion with Christ is being on the way, a permanent ascent toward the true heights of our call. Journeying on together with Jesus is at the same time also a journeying on in the "we" of those who want to follow him. It introduces us into this community. Since the way to true life, to being people in conformity with the model of the Son of God Jesus Christ, surpasses our own strength, this journey always means being carried. We find ourselves, so to speak, roped to Jesus Christ together with him on the ascent towards God's heights. He pulls and supports us. It is part of following Christ that we allow ourselves to be roped together; that we acknowledge we cannot do it alone. This act of humility, entering into the "we" of the Church is part of it; holding tight to the rope, the responsibility of communion not breaking the rope through stubbornness or self-importance. Humbly believing, with the Church, like being a roped-party on the ascent towards God, is an essential condition for the following of Christ. This being roped together also entails not behaving as masters of the Word of God, not running after a mistaken idea of emancipation. The humility of "being with" is essential for the ascent. The fact that in the Sacraments we always let the Lord once again take us by the hand is also part of it; that we let ourselves be purified and strengthened by him; that we accept the discipline of the ascent, even when we are weary.

Discipline and self-sacrifice

Lastly, we must say again: the Cross is also part of the ascent towards the heights of Jesus Christ, of the ascent to the heights of God. Just as in the affairs of this world it is impossible to achieve great results without self-sacrifice and hard work; just as joy in a great discovery of knowledge or in a true operational skill is linked to discipline, indeed, to the effort of learning, so the way toward life itself, to the realization of one's own humanity, is linked to communion with the One who ascended to God's heights through the Cross. In the final analysis, the Cross is an expression of what love means: only those who lose themselves find themselves.

One communion

Let us sum up: the following of Christ requires, as a first step, a reawakening of the desire to be authentic human beings and thus the reawakening of oneself for God. It then requires us to join the climbing party, in the communion of the Church. In the "we" of the Church we enter into communion with the "you" of Jesus Christ and thus reach the path to God. We are also asked to listen to the Word of Jesus Christ and to live it: in faith, hope and love. Thus we are on the way toward the definitive Jerusalem and, from this moment, in a certain way, we already find ourselves there, in the communion of all God's Saints...

The fundamental rules of true love

Let us return once again to the Palm Sunday Liturgy. In the prayer with which the palms are blessed, we pray that in communion with Christ we may bear fruit with good works. Subsequent to an erroneous interpretation of St Paul, the opinion that good works are not part of being Christian or in any case are insignificant for the human being's salvation has emerged time and again in the course of history and also today. But if Paul says that works cannot justify man, with this he did not oppose the importance of right action and, if he speaks of the end of the Law, he does not say that the Ten Commandments are obsolete and irrelevant. There is no need now to reflect on the full breadth of the issue that concerned the Apostle. What is important is to point out that with the term "Law" he does not mean the Ten Commandments but rather the complex way of life Israel had adopted to protect itself against the temptations of paganism. Now, however, Christ has brought God to the pagans. This form of distinction was not imposed upon them. They were given as the Law Christ alone. However, this means love of God and of neighbour and of everything that this entails. The Commandments, interpreted in a new and deeper way starting from Christ, are part of this love, those Commandments are none other than the fundamental rules of true love: first of all, and as a fundamental principle, the worship of God, the primacy of God, which the first three Commandments express. They say: "without God nothing succeeds correctly. Who this God is and how he is we know from the person of Jesus Christ. Next come the holiness of the family (4th Commandment), the holiness of life (5th Commandment), the order of marriage (6th Commandment), the social order (7th Commandment), and lastly the inviolability of the truth (8th Commandment). Today all this is of the greatest timeliness and precisely also in St Paul's meaning if we read all his Letters. "Bear fruit with good works": at the beginning of Holy Week let us pray the Lord to grant us this fruit in ever greater abundance.

The place of peace

At the end of the Gospel for the blessing of the palms, we hear the acclamation with which the pilgrims greet Jesus at the Gates of Jerusalem. It takes up the words of Psalm 118 (117), which priests originally proclaimed to pilgrims from the Holy City but which, in the meantime had become an expression of messianic hope: "Blessed is he who enters in the Name of the Lord" (*Ps* 118[117]: 26; cf. Lk 19: 38). Pilgrims see in Jesus the One who is to come in the Name of the Lord. Indeed, according to St Luke's Gospel they insert one more word: "Blessed is the King who comes in the Name of the Lord". And they continue with an acclamation that recalls the message of the Angels at Christmas, but change it in a manner that prompts reflection. The Angels spoke of the glory of God in the highest and of peace on earth among men with whom he was pleased. The pilgrims at the entrance to the Holy City say: "Peace on earth and glory be to God in the highest!". They know only too well that there is no peace on earth. And they know that the place of peace is Heaven they know that it is an essential part of Heaven to be a haven of peace. This acclamation is therefore an expression of profound suffering and, at the same time, a prayer of hope; may the One who comes in the Name of the Lord bring to the earth what there is in Heaven. May his kingship become the kingship of God, the presence of Heaven on earth. The Church, before the Eucharistic consecration, sings the words of the Psalm with which Jesus was greeted before his entry into the Holy City: She greets Jesus as the King who, coming from God, comes among us in the Name of God. Today too, this joyous greeting is always a supplication and hope. Let us pray the Lord that he bring to us Heaven, the glory of God and peace among men. Let us understand this greeting in the spirit of the request in the Our Father: “Thy will be done”. We know that Heaven is Heaven, a place of glory and peace because the will of God totally prevails there. And we know that the earth will not be Heaven as long as God's will is not done on it. Let us therefore greet Jesus who comes down from Heaven and pray him to help us to recognize and to do God's will. May God's kingship enter the world and thus be filled with the splendour of peace. Amen.

Living the days of the Easter Triduum

We are living the holy days that invite us to meditate on the central events of our Redemption, the essential core of our faith. Tomorrow the Easter Triduum begins, the fulcrum of the whole Liturgical Year in which we are called to silence and prayer in order to contemplate the mystery of the Passion, death and Resurrection of the Lord.

In their Homilies the Fathers often referred to these days which, as St Athanasius observed in one of his *Easter Letters*, bring "us to a new beginning, even the announcement of the blessed Passover, in which the Lord was sacrificed" (*Letter* 5, 1-2: PG 26, 1379).

I therefore urge you to live these days intensely, so that they may decisively direct the life of each one to generous and convinced adherence to Christ, who died and rose for us.

Holy Chrism Mass

Tomorrow morning, the Holy Chrism Mass, a morning prelude to Holy Thursday, will see priests gathered with their own Bishop. During an important Eucharistic celebration which usually takes place in the diocesan cathedrals, the oil of the sick and of the catechumens and chrism will be blessed. In addition, the Bishop and Priests will renew the priestly promises that they spoke on the day of their Ordination. This year, this action acquires a very special prominence because it is taking place in the context of the Year for Priests, which I established to commemorate the 150th anniversary of the death of the holy Curé d'Ars. To all priests I would like to repeat the hope I expressed at the end of my Letter for its inauguration: "In the footsteps of the holy Curé of Ars, let yourselves be enthralled by him. In this way you too will be, for the world in our time, heralds of hope, reconciliation and peace!".

Holy Thursday

Tomorrow afternoon we shall celebrate the institution of the Eucharist. Writing to the Corinthians, the Apostle Paul strengthened the early Christians in the truth of the Eucharistic Mystery, conveying to them what he himself had learned. "The Lord Jesus on the night when he was betrayed took bread, and when he had given thanks, he broke it, and said, "This is my Body which is for you. Do this in remembrance of me'. In the same way also the cup, after supper, saying, "This cup is the new covenant in my Blood. Do this, as often as you drink it, in remembrance of me'" (1 *Cor* 11: 23-25).

These words clearly express Christ's intention: under the species of the bread and the wine, he makes himself really present with his Body given and his Blood poured out as a sacrifice of the New Covenant. At the same time, he constitutes the Apostles and their successors ministers of this Sacrament, which he entrusts to his Church as a supreme proof of his love.

We also commemorate with an evocative rite the gesture of Jesus who washes the Apostles' feet (*Jn* 13: 1-25). For the Evangelist this act comes to portray the whole of Jesus' life and reveals his love to the end, an infinite love that is capable of preparing man for communion with God and of setting him free. At the end of the Holy Thursday Liturgy the Church puts the Blessed Sacrament in a specially prepared place that represents Jesus' loneliness and mortal anguish in Gethsemane. Before the Eucharist, the faithful contemplate Jesus in the hour of his solitude and pray that all the loneliness in the world may cease. This liturgical itinerary is likewise an invitation to seek the intimate encounter with the Lord in prayer, to recognize Jesus among those who are lonely, to watch with him and to proclaim him with the light of one's own life.

Good Friday

On Good Friday we shall commemorate the Passion and death of the Lord. Jesus wanted to give his life as a sacrifice for the forgiveness of humanity's sins, choosing to this end the most brutal and humiliating death: crucifixion. There is an inseparable connection between the Last Supper and Jesus' death. At the Last Supper Jesus gives his Body and his Blood, that is, his earthly existence, himself, anticipating his death and transforming it into an act of love. Thus he makes death which by its nature is the end, the destruction of every relationship an act of the communication of himself, a means of salvation and of the proclamation of the victory of love. In this way, Jesus becomes the key to understanding the Last Supper, which is an anticipation of the transformation of violent death into a voluntary sacrifice; into an act of love that redeems and saves the world.

Holy Saturday

Holy Saturday is marked by a profound silence. The Churches are bare and no special Liturgies are planned. In this time of waiting and hope, believers are invited to prayer, reflection and conversion, also by means of the sacrament of Reconciliation, in order to take part, intimately renewed, in the celebration of Easter.

In the night of Holy Saturday, during the solemn Easter Vigil, "mother of all vigils", this silence will be broken by the singing of the *Alleluia* which announces Christ's Resurrection and proclaims the victory of light over darkness, of life over death. The Church will rejoice in the encounter with her Lord, entering Easter Day which the Lord will inaugurate by rising from the dead.

The Oil of Gladness

At the centre of the Church's worship is the notion of "sacrament". This means that it is not primarily we who act, but God comes first to meet us through his action, he looks upon us and he leads us to himself. Another striking feature is this: God touches us through material things, through gifts of creation that he takes up into his service, making them instruments of the encounter between us and himself. There are four elements in creation on which the world of sacraments is built: water, bread, wine and olive oil. Water, as the basic element and fundamental condition of all life, is the essential sign of the act in which, through baptism, we become Christians and are born to new life. While water is the vital element everywhere, and thus represents the shared access of all people to rebirth as Christians, the other three elements belong to the culture of the Mediterranean region. In other words, they point towards the concrete historical environment in which Christianity emerged. God acted in a clearly defined place on the earth, he truly made history with men. On the one hand, these three elements are gifts of creation, and on the other, they also indicate the locality of the history of God with us. They are a synthesis between creation and history: gifts of God that always connect us to those parts of the world where God chose to act with us in historical time, where he chose to become one of us.

Anointed

Within these three elements there is a further gradation. Bread has to do with everyday life. It is the fundamental gift of life day by day. Wine has to do with feasting, with the fine things of creation, in which, at the same time, the joy of the redeemed finds particular expression. Olive oil has a wide range of meaning. It is nourishment, it is medicine, it gives beauty, it prepares us for battle and it gives strength. Kings and priests are anointed with oil, which is thus a sign of dignity and responsibility, and likewise of the strength that comes from God. Even the name that we bear as "Christians" contains the mystery of the oil. The word "Christians", in fact, by which Christ's disciples were known in the earliest days of Gentile Christianity, is derived from the word "Christ" (*Acts* 11:20-21) – the Greek translation of the word "Messiah", which means "anointed one". To be a Christian is to come from Christ, to belong to Christ, to the anointed one of God, to whom God granted kingship and priesthood. It means belonging to him whom God himself anointed – not with material oil, but with the One whom the oil represents: with his Holy Spirit. Olive oil is thus in a very particular way a symbol of the total compenetration of the man Jesus by the Holy Spirit.

Holy oils a central element

In the Chrism Mass on Holy Thursday, the holy oils are at the centre of the liturgical action. They are consecrated in the bishop's cathedral for the whole year. They thus serve also as an expression of the Church's unity, guaranteed by the episcopate, and they point to Christ, the true "shepherd and guardian" of our souls, as Saint Peter calls him (1 *Pet* 2:25). At the same time, they hold together the entire liturgical year, anchored in the mystery of Holy Thursday. Finally, they point to the Garden of Olives, the scene of Jesus' inner acceptance of his Passion. Yet the Garden of Olives is also the place from which he ascended to the Father, and is therefore the place of redemption: God did not leave Jesus in death. Jesus lives forever with the Father, and is therefore omnipresent, with us always. This double mystery of the Mount of Olives is also always "at work" within the Church's sacramental oil. In four sacraments, oil is the sign of God's goodness reaching out to touch us: in baptism, in confirmation as the sacrament of the Holy Spirit, in the different grades of the sacrament of holy orders and finally in the anointing of the sick, in which oil is offered to us, so to speak, as God's medicine – as the medicine which now assures us of his goodness, offering us strength and consolation, yet at the same time points beyond the moment of the illness towards the definitive healing, the resurrection (cf. *Jas* 5:14). Thus oil, in its different forms, accompanies us throughout our lives: beginning with the catechumenate and baptism, and continuing right up to the moment when we prepare to meet God, our Judge and Saviour. Moreover, the Chrism Mass, in which the sacramental sign of oil is presented to us as part of the language of God's creation, speaks in particular to us who are priests: it speaks of Christ, whom God anointed King and Priest – of him who makes us sharers in his priesthood, in his "anointing", through our own priestly ordination.

The oil of mercy in the lamp of our lives

I should like, then, to attempt a brief interpretation of the mystery of this holy sign in its essential reference to the priestly vocation. In popular etymologies a connection was made, even in ancient times, between the Greek word "*elaion*" – oil – and the word "*eleos*" – mercy. In fact, in the various sacraments, consecrated oil is always a sign of God's mercy. So the meaning of priestly anointing always includes the mission to bring God's mercy to those we serve. In the lamp of our lives, the oil of mercy should never run dry. Let us always obtain it from the Lord in good time – in our encounter with his word, in our reception of the sacraments, in the time we spend with him in prayer.

Symbol of peace

As a consequence of the story of the dove bearing an olive branch to signal the end of the flood – and thus God's new peace with the world of men – not only the dove but also the olive branch and oil itself have become symbols of peace. The Christians of antiquity loved to decorate the tombs of their dead with the crown of victory and the olive branch, symbol of peace. They knew that Christ conquered death and that their dead were resting in the peace of Christ. They knew that they themselves were awaited by Christ, that he had promised them the peace which the world cannot give. They remembered that the first words of the Risen Lord to his disciples were: "Peace be with you!" (*Jn* 20:19). He himself, so to speak, bears the olive branch, he introduces his peace into the world. He announces God's saving goodness. He is our peace. Christians should therefore be people of peace, people who recognize and live the mystery of the Cross as a mystery of reconciliation. Christ does not conquer through the sword, but through the Cross. He wins by conquering hatred. He wins through the force of his greater love. The Cross of Christ expresses his "no" to violence. And in this way, it is God's victory sign, which announces Jesus' new way. The one who suffered was stronger than the ones who exercised power. In his self-giving on the Cross, Christ conquered violence. As priests we are called, in fellowship with Jesus Christ, to be men of peace, we are called to oppose violence and to trust in the greater power of love.

Strength for the battle

A further aspect of the symbolism of oil is that it strengthens for battle. This does not contradict the theme of peace, but forms part of it. The battle of Christians consisted – and still consists – not in the use of violence, but in the fact that they were – and are – ready to suffer for the good, for God. It consists in the fact that Christians, as good citizens, keep the law and do what is just and good. It consists in the fact that they do not do whatever within the legal system in force is not just but unjust. The battle of the martyrs consists in their concrete "no" to injustice: by taking no part in idolatry, in Emperor worship, they refused to bow down before falsehood, before the adoration of human persons and their power. With their "no" to falsehood and all its consequences, they upheld the power of right and truth. Thus they served true peace. Today too it is important for Christians to follow what is right, which is the foundation of peace. Today too it is important for Christians not to accept a wrong that is enshrined in law – for example the killing of innocent unborn children. In this way we serve peace, in this way we find ourselves following in the footsteps of Jesus Christ, of whom Saint Peter says: "When he was reviled he did not revile in return; when he suffered, he did not threaten; but he trusted to him who judges justly. He himself bore our sins in his body on the tree, that we might die to sin and live to righteousness" (1 *Pet* 2:23f.).

Gladness is the fruit of love

The Fathers of the Church were fascinated by a phrase from Psalm 45 (44) – traditionally held to be Solomon's wedding psalm – which was reinterpreted by Christians as the psalm for the marriage of the new Solomon, Jesus Christ, to his Church. To the King, Christ, it is said: "Your love is for justice; your hatred for evil. Therefore God, your God, has anointed you with the oil of gladness above other kings" (v. 8). What is this oil of gladness with which the true king, Christ, was anointed? The Fathers had no doubt in this regard: the oil of gladness is the Holy Spirit himself, who was poured out upon Jesus Christ. The Holy Spirit is the gladness that comes from God. From Jesus this gladness sweeps over us in his Gospel, in the joyful message that God knows us, that he is good and that his goodness is the power above all powers; that we are wanted and loved by him. Gladness is the fruit of love. The oil of gladness, which was poured out over Christ and comes to us from him, is the Holy Spirit, the gift of Love who makes us glad to be alive. Since we know Christ, and since in him we know the true God, we know that it is good to be a human being. It is good to be alive, because we are loved, because truth itself is good.

The presence of the Holy Spirit

In the early Church, the consecrated oil was considered a special sign of the presence of the Holy Spirit, who communicates himself to us as a gift from Christ. He is the oil of gladness. This gladness is different from entertainment and from the outward happiness that modern society seeks for itself. Entertainment, in its proper place, is certainly good and enjoyable. It is good to be able to laugh. But entertainment is not everything. It is only a small part of our lives, and when it tries to be the whole, it becomes a mask behind which despair lurks, or at least doubt over whether life is really good, or whether non-existence might perhaps be better than existence. The gladness that comes to us from Christ is different. It does indeed make us happy, but it can also perfectly well coexist with suffering. It gives us the capacity to suffer and, in suffering, to remain nevertheless profoundly glad. It gives us the capacity to share the suffering of others and thus by placing ourselves at one another's disposal, to express tangibly the light and the goodness of God. I am always struck by the passage in the Acts of the Apostles which recounts that after the Apostles had been whipped by order of the Sanhedrin, they "rejoiced that they were counted worthy to suffer dishonour for the name of Jesus" (*Acts* 5:41). Anyone who loves is ready to suffer for the beloved and for the sake of his love, and in this way he experiences a deeper joy. The joy of the martyrs was stronger than the torments inflicted on them. This joy was ultimately victorious and opened the gates of history for Christ. As priests, we are – in Saint Paul's words – "co-workers with you for your joy" (2 *Cor* 1:24). In the fruit of the olive-tree, in the consecrated oil, we are touched by the goodness of the Creator, the love of the Redeemer. Let us pray that his gladness may pervade us ever more deeply and that we may be capable of bringing it anew to a world in such urgent need of the joy that has its source in truth. Amen.

The Words of Jesus at the Last Supper

In his Gospel, Saint John, more fully than the other three evangelists, reports in his own distinctive way the farewell discourses of Jesus; they appear as his testament and a synthesis of the core of his message. They are introduced by the washing of feet, in which Jesus' redemptive ministry on behalf of a humanity needing purification is summed up in this gesture of humility. Jesus' words end as a prayer, his priestly prayer, whose background exegetes have traced to the ritual of the Jewish feast of Atonement. The significance of that feast and its rituals – the world's purification and reconciliation with God – is fulfilled in Jesus' prayer, a prayer which anticipates his Passion and transforms it into a prayer. The priestly prayer thus makes uniquely evident the perpetual mystery of Holy Thursday: the new priesthood of Jesus Christ and its prolongation in the consecration of the Apostles, in the incorporation of the disciples into the Lord's priesthood. From this inexhaustibly profound text, I would like to select three sayings of Jesus which can lead us more fully into the mystery of Holy Thursday.

Eternal life

First, there are the words: "This is eternal life, that they may know you, the only true God, and Jesus Christ, whom you have sent" (*Jn* 17:3). Everyone wants to have life. We long for a life which is authentic, complete, worthwhile, full of joy. This yearning for life coexists with a resistance to death, which nonetheless remains unescapable. When Jesus speaks about eternal life, he is referring to real and true life, a life worthy of being lived. He is not simply speaking about life after death. He is talking about authentic life, a life fully alive and thus not subject to death, yet one which can already, and indeed must, begin in this world. Only if we learn even now how to live authentically, if we learn how to live the life which death cannot take away, does the promise of eternity become meaningful. But how does this happen? What is this true and eternal life which death cannot touch? We have heard Jesus' answer: this is eternal life, that they may know you – God – and the one whom you have sent, Jesus Christ. Much to our surprise, we are told that life is knowledge. This means first of all that life is relationship. No one has life from himself and only for himself. We have it from others and in a relationship with others. If it is a relationship in truth and love, a giving and receiving, it gives fullness to life and makes it beautiful. But for that very reason, the destruction of that relationship by death can be especially painful, it can put life itself in question. Only a relationship with the One who is himself Life can preserve my life beyond the floodwaters of death, can bring me through them alive. Already in Greek philosophy we encounter the idea that man can find eternal life if he clings to what is indestructible – to truth, which is eternal. He needs, as it were, to be full of truth in order to bear within himself the stuff of eternity. But only if truth is a Person, can it lead me through the night of death. We cling to God – to Jesus Christ the Risen One. And thus we are led by the One who is himself Life. In this relationship we too live by passing through death, since we are not forsaken by the One who is himself Life.

Knowledge

But let us return to Jesus's words – this is eternal life: that they know you and the One whom you have sent. Knowledge of God becomes eternal life. Clearly "knowledge" here means something more than mere factual knowledge, as, for example, when we know that a famous person has died or a discovery was made. Knowing, in the language of sacred Scripture, is an interior becoming one with the other. Knowing God, knowing Christ, always means loving him, becoming, in a sense, one with him by virtue of that knowledge and love. Our life becomes authentic and true life, and thus eternal life, when we know the One who is the source of all being and all life. And so Jesus' words become a summons: let us become friends of Jesus, let us try to know him all the more! Let us live in dialogue with him! Let us learn from him how to live aright, let us be his witnesses! Then we become people who love and then we act aright. Then we are truly alive.

Revealing God's name

Twice in the course of the priestly prayer Jesus speaks of revealing God's name. "I have made your name known to those whom you gave me from the world" (v. 6). "I have made your name known to them, and I will make it known, so that the love with which you have loved me may be in them, and I in them" (v. 26). The Lord is alluding here to the scene of the burning bush, when God, at Moses' request, had revealed his name. Jesus thus means to say that he is bringing to fulfilment what began with the burning bush; that in him God, who had made himself known to Moses, now reveals himself fully. And that in doing so he brings about reconciliation; that the love with which God loves his Son in the mystery of the Trinity now draws men and women into this divine circle of love. But what, more precisely, does it mean to say that the revelation made from the burning bush is finally brought to completion, fully attains its purpose? The essence of what took place on Mount Horeb was not the mysterious word, the "name" which God had revealed to Moses, as a kind of mark of identification. To give one's name means to enter into relationship with another. The revelation of the divine name, then, means that God, infinite and self-subsistent, enters into the network of human relationships; that he comes out of himself, so to speak, and becomes one of us, present among us and for us. Consequently, Israel saw in the name of God not merely a word steeped in mystery, but an affirmation that God is with us. According to sacred

Scripture, the Temple is the dwelling-place of God's name. God is not confined within any earthly space; he remains infinitely above and beyond the world. Yet in the Temple he is present for us as the One who can be called – as the One who wills to be with us. This desire of God to be with his people comes to completion in the incarnation of the Son. Here what began at the burning bush is truly brought to completion: God, as a Man, is able to be called by us and he is close to us. He is one of us, yet he remains the eternal and infinite God. His love comes forth, so to speak, from himself and enters into our midst. The mystery of the Eucharist, the presence of the Lord under the appearances of bread and wine, is the highest and most sublime way in which this new mode of God's being-with-us takes shape. "Truly you are a God who is hidden, O God of Israel", the prophet Isaiah had prayed (45:15). This never ceases to be true. But we can also say: Truly you are a God who is close, you are a God-with-us. You have revealed your mystery to us, you have shown your face to us. You have revealed yourself and given yourself into our hands… At this hour joy and gratitude must fill us, because God has shown himself, because he, infinite and beyond the grasp of our reason, is the God who is close to us, who loves us, and whom we can know and love.

Petition for the unity of the disciples

The best-known petition of the priestly prayer is the petition for the unity of the disciples, now and yet to come. The Lord says, "I do not ask only on behalf of these – that is, the community of the disciples gathered in the Upper Room – but also on behalf of those who will believe in me through their word, that they may all be one. As you, Father, are in me, and I am in you, may they also be in us, so that the world may believe that you have sent me" (v. 20ff.; cf. vv. 11 and 13). What exactly is the Lord asking for? First, he prays for his disciples, present and future. He peers into the distance of future history. He sees the dangers there and he commends this community to the heart of the Father. He prays to the Father for the Church and for her unity. It has been said that in the Gospel of John the Church is not present – and it is true that word *ekklesia* is not used by John – and yet she appears here in her essential features: as the community of disciples who through the apostolic preaching believe in Jesus Christ and thus become one. Jesus prays for the Church to be one and apostolic. This prayer, then, is properly speaking an act which founds the Church. The Lord prays to the Father for the Church. She is born of the prayer of Jesus and through the preaching of the Apostles, who make known God's name and introduce men and women into the fellowship of love with God. Jesus thus prays that the preaching of the disciples will continue for all time, that it will gather together men and women who know God and the one he has sent, his Son Jesus Christ. He prays that men and women may be led to faith and, through faith, to love. He asks the Father that these believers "be in us" (v. 21); that they will live, in other words, in interior communion with God and Jesus Christ, and that this inward being in communion with God may give rise to visible unity. Twice the Lord says that this unity should make the world believe in the mission of Jesus. It must thus be a unity which can be seen – a unity which so transcends ordinary human possibilities as to become a sign before the world and to authenticate the mission of Jesus Christ. Jesus' prayer gives us the assurance that the preaching of the Apostles will never fail throughout history; that it will always awaken faith and gather men and women into unity – into a unity which becomes a testimony to the mission of Jesus Christ. But this prayer also challenges us to a constant examination of conscience. At this hour the Lord is asking us: are you living, through faith, in fellowship with me and thus in fellowship with God? Or are you rather living for yourself, and thus apart from faith? And are you not thus guilty of the inconsistency which obscures my mission in the world and prevents men and women from encountering God's love? It was part of the historical Passion of Jesus, and remains part of his ongoing Passion throughout history, that he saw, and even now continues to see, all that threatens and destroys unity. As we meditate on the Passion of the Lord, let us also feel Jesus' pain at the way that we contradict his prayer, that we resist his love, that we oppose the unity which should bear witness before the world to his mission.

Holy Eucharist

At this hour, when the Lord in the most holy Eucharist gives himself, his body and his blood, into our hands and into our hearts, let us be moved by his prayer. Let us enter into his prayer and thus beseech him: Lord, grant us faith in you, who are one with the Father in the Holy Spirit. Grant that we may live in your love and thus become one, as you are one with the Father, so that the world may believe. Amen.

Resurrection Transforms the Cross

This evening, in stillness and moved in heart, we have journeyed in prayer along the Way of the Cross. We have gone up Calvary with Jesus and we have meditated on his suffering, rediscovering how deep his love was and is for us. But let us not limit ourselves to a compassion dictated be weak sentiment; rather, we wish to participate in the sufferings of Jesus, we wish to accompany our Master, to share his Passion in our lives, in the life of the Church, for the life of the world, since we know that it is precisely in the Lord's Cross, in love without limits, that he gives everything of himself, is the source of grace, of liberation, of peace, of salvation.

The texts, the meditations and the prayers of the *Way of the Cross* have helped us to consider the mystery of the Passion in order to appreciate the great lesson of love which God gave on the Cross, that there might be born in us a renewed desire to change our hearts, living each day that love which is the only force able to change the world.

The grain of wheat

This evening we have gazed upon Jesus and his countenance marked by pain, derided, outraged and disfigured by the sin of humanity; tomorrow night we will look upon the same countenance full of joy, radiant and luminous. From the moment Jesus goes into the tomb, the tomb and death are no longer a place without hope where history stops in the most complete failure, where man touches the extreme limit of his powerlessness. Good Friday is the greatest day of hope, come to fruition upon the Cross, as Jesus dies, as he draws his last breath, crying out with a loud voice, "Father, into your hands I commend my spirit" (*Lk* 23:46). Entrusting his "given" existence into the Father's hands, he knows that his death is becoming the source of life, just as the seed in the earth must be destroyed that a new plant may be born: "If a grain of wheat falls into the earth and dies, it remains alone; but if it dies, it bears much fruit" (*Jn* 12:24). Jesus is the grain of wheat that falls to the earth, is split open, is destroyed and dies, and for this very reason is able to bear fruit. From the day on which Christ was raised upon it, the Cross, which had seemed to be a sign of desolation, of abandonment, and of failure, has become a new beginning: from the profundity of death is raised the promise of eternal life. The victorious splendour of the dawning day of Easter already shines upon the Cross.

Boundless love

In the silence of this night, in the silence which envelopes Holy Saturday, touched by the limitless love of God, we live in the hope of the dawn of the third day, the dawn of the victory of God's love, the luminous daybreak which allows the eyes of our heart to see afresh our life, its difficulties, its suffering. Our failures, our disappointments, our bitterness, which seem to signal that all is lost, are instead illumined by hope. The act of love upon the Cross is confirmed by the Father and the dazzling light of the resurrection enfolds and transforms everything: friendship can be born from betrayal, pardon from denial, love from hate.

Grant us, Lord, to carry our cross with love, and to carry our daily crosses in the certainty that they have been enlightened by the dazzling light of Easter. Amen.

The Medicine of Immortality

An ancient Jewish legend from the apocryphal book "*The life of Adam and Eve*" recounts that, in his final illness, Adam sent his son Seth together with Eve into the region of Paradise to fetch the oil of mercy, so that he could be anointed with it and healed. The two of them went in search of the tree of life, and after much praying and weeping on their part, the Archangel Michael appeared to them, and told them they would not obtain the oil of the tree of mercy and that Adam would have to die.

Later, Christian readers added a word of consolation to the Archangel's message, to the effect that after 5,500 years the loving King, Christ, would come, the Son of God who would anoint all those who believe in him with the oil of his mercy. "The oil of mercy from eternity to eternity will be given to those who are reborn of water and the Holy Spirit. Then the Son of God, Christ, abounding in love, will descend into the depths of the earth and will lead your father into Paradise, to the tree of mercy."

This legend lays bare the whole of humanity's anguish at the destiny of illness, pain and death that has been imposed upon us. Man's resistance to death becomes evident: somewhere – people have constantly thought – there must be some cure for death. Sooner or later it should be possible to find the remedy not only for this or that illness, but for our ultimate destiny – for death itself. Surely the medicine of immortality must exist.

Today too, the search for a source of healing continues. Modern medical science strives, if not exactly to exclude death, at least to eliminate as many as possible of its causes, to postpone it further and further, to prolong life more and more. But let us reflect for a moment: what would it really be like if we were to succeed, perhaps not in excluding death totally, but in postponing it indefinitely, in reaching an age of several hundred years? Would that be a good thing? Humanity would become extraordinarily old, there would be no more room for youth. Capacity for innovation would die, and endless life would be no paradise, if anything a condemnation.

The true cure for death must be different. It cannot lead simply to an indefinite prolongation of this current life. It would have to transform our lives from within. It would need to create a new life within us, truly fit for eternity: it would need to transform us in such a way as not to come to an end with death, but only then to begin in fullness. What is new and exciting in the Christian message, in the Gospel of Jesus Christ, was and is that we are told: yes indeed, this cure for death, this true medicine of immortality, does exist. It has been found. It is within our reach. In baptism, this medicine is given to us. A new life begins in us, a life that matures in faith and is not extinguished by the death of the old life, but is only then fully revealed.

A new life that knows no death

To this some, perhaps many, will respond: I certainly hear the message, but I lack faith. And even those who want to believe will ask: but is it really so? How are we to picture it to ourselves? How does this transformation of the old life come about, so as to give birth to the new life that knows no death? Once again, an ancient Jewish text can help us form an idea of the mysterious process that begins in us at baptism. There it is recounted how the patriarch Enoch was taken up to the throne of God. But he was filled with fear in the presence of the glorious angelic powers, and in his human weakness he could not contemplate the face of God. "Then God said to Michael," to quote from the book of Enoch, "'Take Enoch and remove his earthly clothing. Anoint him with sweet oil and vest him in the robes of glory!' And Michael took off my garments, anointed me with sweet oil, and this oil was more than a radiant light … its splendour was like the rays of the sun. When I looked at myself, I saw that I was like one of the glorious beings" (Ph. Rech, *Inbild des Kosmos*, II 524).

Precisely this – being reclothed in the new garment of God – is what happens in baptism, so the Christian faith tells us. To be sure, this changing of garments is something that continues for the whole of life. What happens in baptism is the beginning of a process that embraces the whole of our life – it makes us fit for eternity, in such a way that, robed in the garment of light of Jesus Christ, we can appear before the face of God and live with him forever.

Rite of renunciation removing the garments of death

In the rite of baptism there are two elements in which this event is expressed and made visible in a way that demands commitment for the rest of our lives. There is first of all the rite of renunciation and the promises. In the early Church, the one to be baptized turned towards the west, the symbol of darkness, sunset, death and hence the dominion of sin. The one to be baptized turned in that direction and pronounced a threefold "no": to the devil, to his pomp and to sin. The strange word "pomp", that is to say the devil's glamour, referred to the splendour of the ancient cult of the gods and of the ancient theatre, in which it was considered entertaining to watch people being torn limb from limb by wild beasts. What was being renounced by this "no" was a type of culture that ensnared man in the adoration of power, in the world of greed, in lies, in cruelty. It was an act of liberation from the imposition of a form of life that was presented as pleasure and yet hastened the destruction of all that was best in man. This renunciation – albeit in less dramatic form – remains an essential part of baptism today. We remove the "old garments", which we cannot wear in God's presence. Or better put: we begin to remove them. This renunciation is actually a promise in which we hold out our hand to Christ, so that he may guide us and reclothe us. What these "garments" are that we take off, what the promise is that we make, becomes clear when we see in the fifth chapter of the Letter to the Galatians what Paul calls "works of the flesh" – a term that refers precisely to the old garments that we remove. Paul designates them thus: "fornication, impurity, licentiousness, idolatry, sorcery, enmity, strife, jealousy, anger, selfishness, dissension, party spirit, envy, drunkenness, carousing and the like" (*Gal* 5:19ff.). These are the garments that we remove: the garments of death.

Clothed in the fruits of the spirit

Then, in the practice of the early Church, the one to be baptized turned towards the east – the symbol of light, the symbol of the newly rising sun of history, the symbol of Christ. The candidate for baptism determines the new direction of his life: faith in the Trinitarian God to whom he entrusts himself. Thus it is God who clothes us in the garment of light, the garment of life. Paul calls these new "garments" "fruits of the spirit", and he describes them as follows: "love, joy, peace, patience, kindness, goodness, faithfulness, gentleness, self-control" (*Gal* 5:22).

Rebirth

In the early Church, the candidate for baptism was then truly stripped of his garments. He descended into the baptismal font and was immersed three times – a symbol of death that expresses all the radicality of this removal and change of garments. His former death-bound life the candidate consigns to death with Christ, and he lets himself be drawn up by and with Christ into the new life that transforms him for eternity. Then, emerging from the waters of baptism the neophytes were clothed in the white garment, the garment of God's light, and they received the lighted candle as a sign of the new life in the light that God himself had lit within them. They knew that they had received the medicine of immortality, which was fully realized at the moment of receiving holy communion. In this sacrament we receive the body of the risen Lord and we ourselves are drawn into this body, firmly held by the One who has conquered death and who carries us through death.

In the course of the centuries, the symbols were simplified, but the essential content of baptism has remained the same. It is no mere cleansing, still less is it a somewhat complicated initiation into a new association. It is death and resurrection, rebirth to new life.

Christ is the tree of life

Indeed, the cure for death does exist. Christ is the tree of life, once more within our reach. If we remain close to him, then we have life. Hence, during this night of resurrection, with all our hearts we shall sing the alleluia, the song of joy that has no need of words. Hence, Paul can say to the Philippians: "Rejoice in the Lord always, again I will say, rejoice!" (*Phil* 4:4). Joy cannot be commanded. It can only be given. The risen Lord gives us joy: true life. We are already held for ever in the love of the One to whom all power in heaven and on earth has been given (cf. *Mt* 28:18). In this way, confident of being heard, we make our own the Church's Prayer over the Gifts from the liturgy of this night: Accept the prayers and offerings of your people. With your help may this Easter mystery of our redemption bring to perfection the saving work you have begun in us. Amen.

The First Gift of the Holy Spirit

In the solemn celebration of Pentecost we are invited to profess our faith in the presence and in the action of the Holy Spirit and to invoke his outpouring upon us, upon the Church and upon the whole world. With special intensity, let us make our own the Church's invocation: *Veni, Sancte Spiritus*! It is such a simple and spontaneous invocation, yet also extraordinarily profound, which came first of all from the heart of Christ. The Spirit is indeed the gift that Jesus asked and continues to ask of his Father for his friends; the first and principal gift that he obtained for us through his Resurrection and Ascension into heaven.

Invocation and donation of the Holy Spirit

Today's Gospel passage, which has the Last Supper as its context, speaks to us of this prayer of Christ. The Lord Jesus said to his disciples: "If you love me, you will keep my commandments. And I will pray the Father, and he will give you another Counsellor, to be with you forever" (*Jn* 14: 15-16). Here the praying heart of Jesus is revealed to us, his filial and fraternal heart. This prayer reaches its apex and its fulfilment on the Cross, where Christ's invocation is one with the total gift that he makes of himself, and thus his prayer becomes, so to speak, the very seal of his self-gift out of love of the Father and humanity. Invocation and donation of the Holy Spirit meet, they permeate each other, they become one reality. "And I will pray the Father, and he will give you another Counsellor, to be with you forever". In reality, Jesus' prayers that of the Last Supper and that on the Cross form a single prayer that continues even in heaven, where Christ sits at the right hand of the Father. Jesus, in fact, always lives his intercessional priesthood on behalf of the people of God and humanity and so prays for all of us, asking the Father for the gift of the Holy Spirit.

Reunification triggered by the Spirit

The account of Pentecost in the Book of the Acts of the Apostles we listened to it in the First Reading (cf. *Acts* 2: 1-11) presents the "new course" of the work that God began with Christ's Resurrection, a work that involves mankind, history and the cosmos. The Son of God, dead and Risen and returned to the Father, now breathes with untold energy the divine breath upon humanity, the Holy Spirit. And what does this new and powerful self-communication of God produce? Where there are divisions and estrangement the Paraclete creates unity and understanding. The Spirit triggers a process of reunification of the divided and dispersed parts of the human family. People, often reduced to individuals in competition or in conflict with each other, when touched by the Spirit of Christ open themselves to the experience of communion, which can involve them to such an extent as to make of them a new body, a new subject: the Church. This is the effect of God's work: unity; thus unity is the sign of recognition, the "business card" of the Church throughout her universal history. From the very beginning, from the Day of Pentecost, she speaks all languages. The universal Church precedes the particular Churches, and the latter must always conform to the former according to a criterion of unity and universality. The Church never remains a prisoner within political, racial and cultural confines; she cannot be confused with States nor with Federations of States, because her unity is of a different type and aspires to transcend every human frontier.

A vocation to unity

From this, dear brothers, derives a practical criterion for discerning Christian life: when a person or a community limits itself to its own way of thinking and acting, it is a sign that it has distanced itself from the Holy Spirit. The path of Christians and of the particular Churches must always coincide with the path of the one, catholic Church, and harmonize with it. This does not mean that the unity created by the Holy Spirit is a kind of egalitarianism. On the contrary, that is rather the model of Babel, or in other words, the imposition of a culture characterized by what we could define as "technical" unity. In fact, the Bible tells us (cf. *Gen* 11: 1-9) that in Babel everyone spoke the same language. At Pentecost, however, the Apostles speak different languages in such a way that everyone understands the message in his own tongue. The unity of the Spirit is manifest in the plurality of understanding. The Church is one and multiple by her nature, destined as she is to live among all nations, all peoples, and in the most diverse social contexts. She responds to her vocation to be a sign and instrument of unity of the human race (cf. *Lumen gentium*, n. 1) only if she remains autonomous from every State and every specific culture. Always and everywhere the Church must truly be catholic and universal, the house of all in which each one can find a place.

Universality

The account of the Acts of the Apostles offers us another very concrete indication. The universality of the Church is expressed by the list of peoples according to the ancient tradition: We are "Parthians, Medes, Elamites", etc. Here one may observe that St Luke goes beyond the number 12, which itself always expresses a universality. He looks beyond the horizons of Asia and northwest Africa, and adds three other elements: the "Romans", that is, the Western world; the "Jews and proselytes", encompassing in a new way the unity between Israel and the world; and finally "Cretans and Arabians", who represent the West and the East, islands and land. This opening of horizons subsequently confirms the newness of Christ in the dimension of human space, in the history of the nations. The Holy Spirit involves individuals and peoples and, through them, overcomes walls and barriers.

A vocation to truth and love

At Pentecost the Holy Spirit is manifest as fire. The Spirit's flame descended upon the assembled disciples, it was kindled in them and gave them the new ardour of God. Thus what Jesus had previously said was fulfilled: "I came to cast fire upon the earth; and would that it were already kindled!" (*Lk* 12: 49). The Apostles, together with diverse communities of the faithful, carried this divine flame to the far corners of the earth. In this way they opened a path for humanity, a luminous path, and they collaborated with God, who wants to renew the face of the earth with his fire. How different is this fire from that of war and bombing! How different is the fire of Christ, spread by the Church, compared with those lit by the dictators of every epoch of the last century too who leave scorched earth behind them. The fire of God, the fire of the Holy Spirit, is that of the bush that burned but was not consumed (cf. Ex 3: 2). It is a flame that blazes but does not destroy, on the contrary, that, in burning, brings out the better and truer part of man, as in a fusion it elicits his interior form, his vocation to truth and to love.

Whoever is near to me, is near to the fire

A Father of the Church, Origen, in one of his Homilies on Jeremiah, cites a saying attributed to Jesus, not contained in the sacred Scriptures but perhaps authentic, which reads: "Whoever is near to me, is near to the fire" (*Homily on Jeremiah*, L. I [III]). In Christ, in fact, there is the fullness of God, who in the Bible is compared to fire. We just observed that the flame of the Holy Spirit blazes but does not burn. And nevertheless it enacts a transformation, and thus must also consume something in man, the waste that corrupts him and hinders his relations with God and neighbour. This effect of the divine fire, however, frightens us; we are afraid of being "scorched" and prefer to stay just as we are. This is because our life is often based on the logic of having, of possessing and not the logic of self-gift. Many people believe in God and admire the person of Jesus Christ, but when they are asked to lose something of themselves, then they retreat; they are afraid of the demands of faith. There is the fear of giving up something pleasant to which we are attached; the fear that following Christ deprives us of freedom, of certain experiences, of a part of ourselves. On the one hand, we want to be with Jesus, follow him closely, and, on the other, we are afraid of the consequences entailed.

Touched by God's flame

Dear brothers and sisters, we are always in need of hearing the Lord Jesus tell us what he often repeated to his friends: "Be not afraid". Like Simon Peter and the others we must allow his presence and his grace to transform our heart, which is always subject to human weakness. We must know how to recognize that losing something indeed, losing ourselves for the true God, the God of love and of life is actually gaining ourselves, finding ourselves more fully. Whoever entrusts himself to Jesus already experiences in this life the peace and joy of heart that the world cannot give, and that it cannot even take away once God has given it to us. So it is worthwhile to let ourselves be touched by the fire of the Holy Spirit! The suffering that it causes us is necessary for our transformation. It is the reality of the Cross. It is not without reason that in the language of Jesus "fire" is above all a representation of the mystery of the Cross, without which Christianity does not exist. Thus enlightened and comforted by these words of life, let us lift up our invocation: Come, Holy Spirit! Enkindle in us the fire of your love! We know that this is a bold prayer, with which we ask to be touched by God's flame; but above all we know that this flame and it alone has the power to save us.

Sources

This booklet draws together homilies and addresses of Pope Benedict XVI made during Lent, Eastertide and Pentecost 2010:

Meeting the Justice of God in Jesus Christ: Message of His Holiness Benedict XVI for Lent 2010, 30 October 2009.

The Birth of a New Nature in us: General Audience, Ash Wednesday, 17 February 2010.

A Universal Desire for Life: "Statio" and penitential procession, homily of His Holiness Benedict XVI, Ash Wednesday, 17 February 2010.

Spiritual Renewal in Lent: Angelus, First Sunday of Lent, 21 February 2010; and Angelus, Second Sunday of Lent, 28 February 2010.

The Way of Repentance: Eucharistic Celebration, homily of His Holiness Benedict XVI, Third Sunday of Lent, 7 March 2010.

Our Relationship with God: Angelus, Fourth Sunday of Lent, 14 March 2010; and Angelus, Fifth Sunday of Lent, 21 March 2010.

The Rules of Love: Celebration of Palm Sunday of the Passion of Our Lord, homily of His Holiness Benedict XVI, 25th World Youth Day, 28 March 2010.

Living the Days of the Easter Triduum: General Audience, Saint Peter's Square, Holy Wednesday, 31 March 2010, Easter Triduum.

The Oil of Gladness: Chrism Mass homily of His Holiness Benedict XVI, Saint Peter's Basilica, Holy Thursday, 1st April 2010.

The Words of Jesus at the Last Supper: Mass of the Lord's Supper, homily of His Holiness Benedict XVI, Basilica of St John Lateran, Holy Thursday, 1st April 2010.

Resurrection Transforms the Cross: Way of the Cross at the Colosseum, Address of His Holiness Benedict XVI, Palatine Hill, Good Friday, 2 April 2010.

The Medicine of Immortality: Easter Vigil, homily of His Holiness Benedict XVI, Saint Peter's Basilica, Holy Saturday, 3 April 2010.

The First Gift of the Holy Spirit: Eucharistic Celebration on the Solemnity of Pentecost, homily of His Holiness Benedict XVI, St Peter's Basilica, Sunday, 23 May 2010.

A world of Catholic reading at your fingertips ...

CTS

... now online

Browse 500 titles at

www.cts-online.org.uk

Catholic Faith, Life, and Truth for all

CTS